MW01286983

The Gardener Philosophy

How to Lead (Worship) Like Jesus

JARED FUJISHIN

ISBN-13: 978-1502343666
ISBN-10: 1502343665

DEDICATION

To my beautiful mother Vicky and amazing father Randy. Thank you for raising me in the ways of the Lord and teaching me what a life modeled after Christ looks like.

To my dearest brother Tyler. Thanks for your friendship and partnership in ministry. Yousss myyy duuuddeeee.

CONTENTS

ACKNOWLEDGMENTS

A special thank you to Brittany Overbeck, Emily Landstrom, Aurora Alarcon, Vicky Fujishin, Tyler Fujishin and Randy Fujishin for all their help with this book.

I would also not be where I am today without the help, love and mentorship of these amazing men and women of God. Thank you to Brandon Yip, Brittany Overbeck, Dr. Bryce Jessup, Dr. Daniel Gluck, Dennis Nichols, Eric Hogue, Eric Swanson-Dexel, Gene De Young, Dr. Glen Gibson, Jim Crain, Jim Jessup, Dr. John Jackson, Lee Fields, Dr. Paul Blezien, Ray Johnston, Steve Richardson, Tom Ruscica, and the personal mentorship and love from Pastors: Fred Hennes, Jeff Lane, Lance Hahn, Rene Schlaepfer, Rob Baker, Ryan Pryor, and Van Cummings.

A big thank you to Andy Stanley and Rick Warren for their massive influence on my leadership life and this book. I have learned so much from their wisdom (and if you are ever reading this, this is my official invitation to coffee, ON ME! I want to meet you guys!)

Finally, a huge shout out to my cousin and dear friend Jon Yetter for the beautiful cover art.

Section 1
The Foundation

1 THE GARDENER PHILOSOPHY

There are five words that completely changed how I saw leadership—five words that changed how I would forever lead worship.

They are found at the end of the book of John, but my guess is that you will not find this verse on a bumper sticker and you will not hear this verse quoted at weddings or funerals. In fact, up until this point, you may have not ever given these words a second thought.

You may have grown up in church your whole life, you may have read the resurrection story a million times, and, if you are anything like me, you probably never even noticed these five words! But the implications and potential impact they hold for your life are too great to capture in words.

They may very well be the most important five words you take from this book and, once explained, you will never read the resurrection story the same, and hopefully, never lead worship the same either. The five words are:

"...thinking he was the gardener" (John 20:15).

Disappointed? Confused? Getting ready to put this book down and write me off? I would probably be having the same thoughts, but please, you've come this far, humor me for one more page. Allow me to explain myself before you dismiss what may very well forever change the way you lead your life, your team, and your congregation in worship!

The hundreds of pages that lead up to this statement set the background for one of the most epic tales of all mankind. If you are a worship leader, you know it by heart. But you may know it so well you missed something...

Here's what you likely DO know: mankind fell, absolutely cut off and separated from God with no hope of salvation...and then Jesus came—a breath of fresh air after 39 books of Old Testament law and human failure. Jesus finally appears and lives the perfect life, and then does the impossible. He beats death at death's own game. And in the moment he rises, he forever changes history, opening up salvation to all mankind.

Can you imagine what that first breath must have been like for all of heaven? Jesus had just done the impossible, the unspeakable, he had become the Name above all names; he had forever changed all of history with that first breath he took in his resurrected body. It was the greatest moment in history.

We talk about it to this day. If anyone was ever deserving of glory, if anyone was ever deserving of attention and the spotlight, it was Jesus at that moment. But in that very moment come the five words that are going to change your life, the five words that will change how you lead and how you live. Are you ready? By John's account, it happened like this:

> Now Mary stood outside the tomb crying. As she
> wept, she bent over to look into the tomb [12] and
> saw two angels in white, seated where Jesus' body
> had been, one at the head and the other at the
> foot. [13] They asked her, "Woman, why are you
> crying?" "They have taken my Lord away," she
> said, "and I don't know where they have put
> him." [14] At this, she turned around and saw Jesus
> standing there, but she did not realize that it was
> Jesus.[15] He asked her, "Woman, why are you
> crying? Who is it you are looking for?" Thinking
> he was the gardener, she said, "Sir, if you have
> carried him away, tell me where you have put
> him, and I will get him." [16] Jesus said to her,
> "Mary." She turned toward him and cried out in
> Aramaic, "Rabboni!" (John 20:11-16 NIV)

Did you catch that? **On his most victorious day in
history, there was something about Jesus that got him
mistaken for a gardener.**

Maybe there was something in his voice, or in his
attire, or maybe it was just the overall way he carried
himself. But on the most glorious day in history, the only
man who truly was deserving of glory came back and
carried himself in such a fashion that people would walk by
him and mistake him for a gardener. A lowly gardener.

If you are anything like me, you are feeling pretty silly
right about now as you think back to all the times you've
tried to get glory for things that are far less impressive than

redeeming all mankind in a single breath. I once led worship for Francis Chan and thought I was hot stuff. I crafted my tweets and Instagram pictures in such a way to appear humorous and humble, but in the end, knew the primary point was to show off, to put the spotlight on me and get the attention I felt I deserved.

I remember times when I first started leading worship and would look in the mirror until I found just the right length to let my in-ears dangle out to look as cool as possible; my end goal being that people would notice me. Then I read this passage and think, dang. Jesus, who was fully deserving of glory and attention, carried himself in such a way he wasn't even recognized by dear friends, he was even mistaken for one of the lowest position in their day. Then along I come, doing things far less impressive than saving mankind, and all I do is try to get all the attention I can. Something is not right.

When I read this, it changed me. It changed how I led worship; it changed how I carried myself, and changed how I trained other leaders. I now aspire to be mistaken for a gardener (or stagehand, roadie, etc.). In my experience, the gardener lifestyle is not only biblical, it also yields far better results in worship and the receptiveness of an audience. It was the way leaders were designed to lead. Jesus modeled this lifestyle to us in the most glorious moment in history.

Over the years I have been leading worship and traveling to different churches, I have discovered some behaviors and practical ways to implement this gardener philosophy. I want to share a few of those with you. But first, we must address a key question... do you really want to lead?

Do You Really Want To Lead?

My grandfather was a gardener for 35 years. Grandpa Mike would wake up at 4 a.m. six days a week to mow lawns, lay fertilizer, and clean up after his upper middle class neighbors.

Let me tell you, the gardener life is not a glamorous one. No one walked by my grandfather secretly envying him for his position. If my grandfather had had social media back then and posted a picture of his daily activities and hard work as a gardener, no one would "like" or "retweet" his photos. No one would comment on his posts. There would be no hidden envy or resentment in his friends as they looked at the things he did. The gardener life is not one that is envied.

Why then, are so many worship leaders' lives envied by the masses in the Christian community today? Why, when you see your favorite musician post a picture of a sold out arena with lights flashing and the sound system bumpin', do you secretly wish you were them? Why do you then compensate by posting pictures and posts of your own as you lead your own service in hopes of making others envy your own life?

The gardener leadership life is not one that is envied, *but the life of a rock star is*. Before you continue, you might want to ask yourself…Do I want to be an effective worship leader, who models my leadership after the example of Christ? Or do I want to be a rock star who is envied by my peers?

We all know the "right" answer here, but I'm not asking for the "right" answer. I'm asking for your true answer. The beauty of where you are right now is that no one can read your thoughts. You may be sitting on a couch, reading this on your phone in an airport, or at your desk skimming this book before walking to your next meeting. The point is, it's just you. It is a safe place to be honest with your true heart's desire.

In this moment, it's just you and the Holy Spirit who already knows your heart. So take a minute before you read this list, and ask The Spirit to humble you and open your eyes to any ugly truths you may hold in your heart or spirit. Once they are revealed to you, ask him to rid you of any impurities of leading from the position of a rock star instead of a humble gardener. Truly ask yourself…Do my actions communicate to myself and others that I want to be a rock star, or a gardener?

ROCK STARS expect to be served by others.
GARDENERS come expecting to serve others.

ROCK STARS do what is best for themselves.
GARDENERS do what is best for the group as a whole.

ROCK STARS expect things setup when they arrive.
GARDENERS come early to help the tech crew set up.

ROCK STARS feel entitled to respect and appreciation.
GARDENERS feel entitled to nothing.

ROCK STARS are full of themselves.
GARDENERS are full of the Spirit.

ROCK STARS spend more time picking their clothes for the morning than praying for the service.
GARDENERS are constantly in communication with our Father.

ROCK STARS talk more about their equipment and the music than the presence of God.
GARDENERS constantly redirect attention back onto the purpose of why they worship.

ROCK STARS are selfish.
GARDENERS are selfless.

ROCK STARS enjoy being built up.
GARDENERS enjoy building others up

Think about this: why did Satan fall from heaven? Isaiah tells us that Satan said in his heart, "I will ascend to heaven; above the stars of God. I will set my throne on high; I will sit on the mount of assembly, in the far reaches of the North. I will ascend above the heights of the clouds, I will make myself like the most high" (Isaiah 14:12-14).

Satan wanted to become greater, he wanted to be seen, he wanted more attention, and he thought he deserved more than he had!

Contrast that with the character of Jesus. Paul tells us that, "[Christ] who, being in very nature God, did not consider equality with God something to be used to his own advantage; rather, he made himself nothing by taking the very nature of a servant...and humbled himself by becoming obedient to death—even death on a cross! Therefore, God exalted him to the highest place" (Philippians 2:6-9).

Jesus, who unlike Satan had every right to come in glory, decided to come humbly. He wanted to become less, he wanted to take the lowly position of a servant, and didn't mind if he did not get the respect he (actually) deserved from all mankind while he was on earth!

After reading both of these descriptions, which does your life look more like? Which of the two do you think would create a culture which forced people to call them by official titles as opposed to just first names? Which of the two do you think would have their profile picture be of them onstage playing their instrument? Which of the two do you think would come just in time to walk onstage versus coming early in "work clothes" prepared to get their hands dirty with a change of clothes in the back?

It frightens me beyond belief, but all too often I see worship leaders (myself included!) looking more and more like Satan in their desires and characteristics and less and less like the Philippians 2 example we have of Christ!

This book will continue to address this issue, and how we can begin to remedy and repair our worship culture from being one of "rock stars" to one of Gardeners, but let me be clear, the gardener philosophy does not give you permission to neglect the pursuit of excellence.

A Spirit of Excellence

Do not confuse the spirit of servanthood with a lack of effort or laziness. Just because you subscribe to the philosophy of humility in leadership does not mean you cannot be an authority in your field or a master of your instrument. It is not one at the expense of the other—it is a "BOTH/AND" kind of thing.

The Lord calls us to excellence. Paul commands us, "Whatever you do, do it with all your heart as if doing it for the Lord and not for man" (Colossians 3:23). Worship leaders should be the trailblazers of musical innovation and remarkable in their skills as a means of bringing glory to our God.

Musical ability is a huge necessity in leading worship, we all know that! I do not want to downplay the importance of excellence. I want to go on record saying excellence should be pursued with all you have and should be a *continual* pursuit.

With that said, this book is not designed to focus on that aspect of the worship leading life. This book is primarily focused on the side of leading worship that I believe is often neglected, overlooked, or not known by many in my field.

What follows in this book are the insights and thoughts I had after traveling the west coast, working alongside numerous churches (big and small) and spending time in worship cultures of all denominations. And I believe, if applied correctly, The Gardener Philosophy will change your personal life, your team dynamics, and your body of worshiping believers.

Section 2
Creating the Ideal Team

2 PEOPLE ARE MIRRORS

The reason the gardener mentality is so crucial to your foundation of leadership is because you replicate who you are, not what you want others to be. If you want quality teams and a quality atmosphere of worship for your church, you need to understand that it starts with you.

You set the tone. Your actions speak loudly, but the people who work with you closely see through the fake, which is why you must internalize and completely live the gardener life, on and off-stage. The atmosphere and culture of your team and your congregation will directly mirror who you are as a person. Be a gardener, not a rock star.

Part of being a gardener takes understanding that worship leading goes far beyond just singing songs onstage. I would go as far as to say that 80% of what you do as a worship leader is done *offstage*. People often only see the 10% of what you do that takes place in those four songs you play onstage on Sunday morning. Perhaps a few more recognize the 10% of the time you allot to set list planning, stage setup, and rehearsal times you put in.

But if you are leading as a quality gardener leader, that is only the tip of the iceberg. There is 80% of living a worship leader's life that is often ignored. That 80% is where the gardener mentality comes in.

What people will likely never see and will never give you credit or praise for is the less glamorous, less flashy 80% of your work that ENABLES the 10% everyone sees to be amazing and well received. If you can learn to do well the things that make up this 80%, the 10% that the congregation takes part in will never be the same. You will see dramatic improvements and significant results.

Similar to how any Joe Shmoe can recognize the beauty in a Mona Lisa painting, even though they may not be able to articulate the brush stroke style or the medium used that makes it beautiful, they see the beauty in the final product. The same is true of investing in this 80% offstage work. It will make the 10% people do see onstage remarkable.

The people in the congregation may not even be able to articulate why they love the worship so much. But even if they don't understand all the steps it took you to get them to that place, the end product will be recognized by the masses all the same. A perfect example of a leader who implements well this 80% of the unseen iceberg is King David from the Old Testament.

David's Mighty Men

King David was not a perfect man. He had his flaws and faults like any of us, but he is the phenomenal example of how the Lord can use broken people (like David and like us) to be amazing leaders.

Here is why I believe David is one of the most inspiring leaders in the Old Testament: he took a group of miscellaneous, independent outcasts and brought them together, all the while creating a culture of great unity among them (1 Chronicles 11:10.) These men were called The 300.

These 300 men were not your ordinary, everyday kind of men. They were not the people who needed a group for safety. If you are looking for quality teams in the Bible, these 300 of David's mighty men make up one of the most impressive ones in the entire Bible. David had people like Jashobeam and Benaiah following him.

Jashobeam, or Joshy as I like to call him (and am sure he would have enjoyed being called that himself) is the kinda guy you only see in movies, the kind of guy you hear stories about around a campfire. The Bible doesn't describe Joshy's physical characteristics, but I like to picture him as a Russell Crowe from The Gladiator mixed with Gerard Butler from the movie 300 and a little Bruce Willis from Die Hard thrown in for good measure. I picture a man with a shaved head, muscles on muscles, and the kind of war cry that could make even the toughest man you know cower in fear (11:11).

Joshy is known for this: he took on 300 men in one encounter and single-handedly slaughtered them all. Don't gloss over this. Single-handedly. I was once accidentally punched in the face by a man who was formerly in the Marines, and let me tell you, I was down for the count. In that moment I learned very quickly I am not cut out for war or violence of any kind. Now imagine going up against 300 men. No guns, no automatic weapons, just swords and fists. Brotha be doing WORK!

Then you have Benaiah, or Benihana as I like to call him (and also just happens to be one of my favorite restaurants for special occasions). Now Benihana is a strange, strange man, but someone who I would want on my team in battle. In addition to being David's personal bodyguard, he is most famous for going down into a pit on a snowy day and killing a lion (11:22).

What? First of all, who kills a lion? Second of all, who goes after a lion? Third of all, who chases a lion into a dark den where the lion has the home court advantage and tries to fight it? What did the lion do to disrespect Benihana to such a degree he felt it was necessary to chase it through the snow into its home turf to fight that fierce little kitty?

I cannot think of a stranger story in scripture, and it comes with no explanation, but you know Benihana was famous after that one. You know he was the guy in the camp every one murmured about when he walked by "Yea, yea, that's the dude that chased a lion into its DEN on a SNOWY DAY and slayed it!!"

The list of David's mighty warriors goes on, but you get the idea. The people that surround David are no interns. They aren't the water boys or the last resort; these guys are the crème of the crop and the kind of men you want beside you in battle. They are the guys you don't want to lose in battle or send on a frivolous mission, and that is what makes the story of 1 Chronicles 11 so interesting.

Usually when you have such strong warriors like the ones David had, you would expect a spirit of competition among them. You may even expect to see some of the warriors be secretly resentful of David and his position of power, his influence, and his authority. You may expect to hear grumbling in the camp and phrases like, "I wouldn't have done it like that" or "When I am the leader..." But that is not what we see in Scripture. In fact, we see quite the opposite!

Three of David's best men make their way down to the Cave of Adullam while a company of Philistines was camped in the Valley of Rephaim and the Philistine garrison was at Bethlehem. David was holed up in the cave while the Philistines were preparing for battle at Bethlehem, when all of the sudden, David had a craving: "What I wouldn't give for a drink of water from the well in Bethlehem, the one at the gate!" (1Chronicles 11:15-17; Message).

The response of his followers gets me every time. The response of his mighty men shows how much they love David. Scripture goes on to tell us, "The Three penetrated the Philistine camp, drew water from the well at the Bethlehem gate, shouldered it, and brought it to David" (1Chronicles 11:18; Message).

Three men broke through an entire army of the enemy to get their leader what he longed for, risked their lives to please David, and gave up everything willingly to make him happy. Sounds like an ideal team, huh? You may experience a surge of jealousy as you contemplate David's team...you are not alone.

When I first read this, I thought to myself, "Why did David get all the best followers?" These guys were David's A-List men. Why did three of the best out of the elite 300 come to find David, listen to all his needs, and then act quickly upon everything he said, risking everything they had just to please their leader?

Was it just luck that those amazing followers fell into David's lap? Or was it something in the way David led? Something in the way he interacted with his followers that made them love and want to serve him in this way?

When you see a great team, understand that nine times out of ten it speaks more to the leadership of the men and women leading than to the natural character of those being led. People are mirrors of you. The people under you, the people who God has entrusted and placed under *your care*, will mirror the manner in which you treat them. David's men were willing to risk their lives and were for *him* because they knew he was for *them*.

The story finishes with a strange ending that again speaks to David's leadership style that goes above and beyond (modeling what the other 80% of that iceberg type of leadership looks like!) After the mighty men risk everything to get David the drink he desires, he doesn't drink it. In fact, he pours the water his men just risked their lives to get (because he said he wanted it) out on the ground!

At this point I'm thinking, how upset would I be if I were one of the mighty men. "Hey Dave, I just risked my life to get you your water, and you're going to pour it on the ground? In front of us?!" But after a little more research and reading, I found what David was doing here was probably one of the reasons the men loved him so much as a leader.

"David poured the water out as a sacred offering saying, 'I'd rather be damned by God than drink this! It would be like drinking the lifeblood of these men—they risked their lives to bring it.' So he refused to drink it." (1Chronicles 11:19; Message). It was a sacred tradition to show a great respect to his men. His relationship with his men was one of mutual respect, modeled from the top down. He communicated with that action that he was for them, and how can you not be for someone who is for you?

As a leader, you need to understand this principle. *The way you interact with those under you, even in the smallest of things, creates a culture.* In the act of pouring out the water, David was creating a culture. Would it have made him a "bad" leader to drink it? No. But the question we should be asking ourselves is not "Will I be a *bad* leader if I _____?" The question we need to learn to ask is, "What would a GREAT leader do in my situation?" and then do that.

As a worship leader, every time you make someone under you go get you a cord rather than getting it yourself, or make the newest guy go get you your water, you are communicating a culture to them. Of course you have no ill intent, you are not thinking you are entitled or deserve to be served. In fact most of the time this happens without us thinking twice about it.

We, as worship leaders, are dealing with the pressures of people from the congregation complaining about the song selection or the noise volume, while trying to keep the sound techs, additional singers, drummer and guitar players happy, as well as trying to get everyone their respective chord charts and make sure everything is up and running, and you just need water! Doesn't it make sense that someone else grabs it for you? Isn't it okay to ask him to get you water?

No. The people under you don't know all the pressures and stresses you are under that dictate your time. The rest of the worship team watching from the outside do not know the stressful meeting you just got out of where you went to bat for them and stood up for them. All they see is you asking the new guy to get you water, and with that one small action, you begin to create a culture. The culture you are creating and communicating, whether directly or indirectly, is that people under you are there to serve you.

Three years ago I was working under a worship leader named Jeff. It was the week leading up to Easter Sunday and things at the church were crazy! People were stressed and tempers were high. It was the Wednesday before Easter and the stage was completely stripped of everything.

Most worship leaders would be tuning and running through songs while the interns set up the entire stage, but not Jeff. Jeff had his button up shirt nicely folded over a chair and was getting his hands (and undershirt) dirty as he crawled around under the stage laying cords. In that moment, he helped set a culture. The culture he was modeling was…we are here to serve, not to be served. From the top down, it was clear that servanthood was an unspoken expectation by all.

We Were Never Called to "Easy"

Being a leader is not fair. You have to think twice as hard about every action you do because your actions set the culture and example on how to lead, all the while creating the legacy of how that operation will run after you leave. It's not easy, but we as leaders were never called to easy. We were called to a higher standard; we were called to something that few can do well. We were called to lead worship on and off-stage. We were called to be gardeners.

So other than modeling servanthood by example, what other practical things can you be doing to evoke the kind of response David's Mighty Men gave to him? What tangible "action item" things can you begin doing to build a culture among your team that brings about a healthy loyalty and a tight-knit bond that cannot be broken?

The following chapter will start you on a path of easy ways to encourage your team. The natural response to encouragement will be a culture like the one King David had with his men. The next chapter will teach you how to "pour out the proverbial water" like David did to show your team honor and respect, resulting in astounding attitude and culture change amidst your team.

3 HOW TO ENCOURAGE YOUR TEAM
(The Power of a 3x5)

We all long for encouragement, but rarely get it. For example, did anyone compliment you on your shirt today? If I had to guess, I would say no one has complimented you on the shirt you are wearing right now and you're probably not expecting anyone to compliment you on your shirt today. Why? Because encouragement is rare.

But can you remember when you bought the shirt you are wearing right now? Look down at your shirt, try to remember when you first saw it in the department store. Something about it struck you enough to make you try it on. Then after you had looked at yourself in the mirror a few times, you thought it made you look good enough to drop some money on it. Remember? Remember how much time and energy went into purchasing the shirt you are wearing right now? And no one complimented you on it today. Encouragement is rare, so rare in fact we no longer expect it from others.

While we know encouragement is desired but rare, we

also know the more rare or unlikely a thing is, the more it's valued. Knowing this puts you in a very powerful position as a leader. Do not miss this—*people are starved for affection, attention, and encouragement.* It is how God designed us as humans and how He keeps us in community, but somewhere along the way we became so focused on ourselves we forgot how to invest in others. We forgot how to speak life into our fellow brothers and sisters, and it has created a deep thirst in the hearts and souls of humanity.

So how do you remedy this? How do you overcome the self-centered nature of the flesh and learn to once again speak life into those around us and encourage others? The answer is quite simple.

I call it **The Golden Gardener Rule**: *imagine what you wish someone would do you for right now...now go do that very thing for someone else.* It is just a matter of learning to use your natural self-centered thoughts as a fuel for selfless actions!

I was walking through the common area near our apartment complex on campus a while back when someone stopped me just to tell me that my hat looked "dope sauce" (...which I am choosing to believe is a compliment:) The guy smiled, gave me a high five, and went on his way.

The whole interaction took less than 10 seconds, but it put me in a great mood for the rest of the day! That guy could have just walked to class and remained in his own world, but he chose to step out from his own little bubble, be aware of his surroundings, and go the extra mile to engage me in conversation and connect with me through the form of an encouraging statement.

What would be encouraging to you as a leader? What

if, when you walked into your rehearsal this week, one of your musicians pulled you aside and told you this, "You know, this week I couldn't help but pray for you! Last time we talked you told me about _____, and I wanted to let you know it was on my mind and heart and I have been praying for you about that, as well for you as my leader and for protection from all attacks of the enemy!"

How much would it bless you to know you were noticed, appreciated, and covered in prayer by one of your team members? Wouldn't you love the person who took the time and energy to do that for you? And over time, if they were consistent, wouldn't that be the kind of person you were loyal to above all else because of how "for you" they proved to be?

I want you to hold onto that feeling of longing you have in you right now, the feeling of "I wish I had a team member who cared for me enough to actually do something kind and thoughtful for me on a weekly basis." Visualize it. Cherish it.

Now, after you have allowed the feeling to flow through you for a moment, remember The Golden Gardener Rule of how to be a blessing *(imagine what you wish someone would do you for right now…now go do that very thing for someone else)* and remember they are not here for you, YOU are here for THEM!

You are entitled to *nothing*; you are simply a gardener who is here to serve others with everything you have. Now if the notion of someone doing all that praying and thanksgiving over you on a weekly basis was encouraging to you, *that's a pretty good indicator you need to be doing it for your team.*

But let's go a step further. Any leader can say nice things to team members or tell them they have been praying for them, but we are going to do something that makes you stand out above the rest. Saying nice things is relatively simple, and because it is so simple, it does not hold as much weight as what I am going to suggest.

I suggest that once a week you take time to write each team member an *encouragement card* on a 3x5 index card that is *unique to him or her*. Then go to sound check early and place those 3x5 cards on the ground where each respective musician will be standing so it is the first thing that greets them! These cards should contain things like:

1. Specific prayers for them
2. Compliments
3. Words of affirmation

Worth the Extra Effort

Two years ago I filled in at a church for a friend who was out of town and implemented these 3x5 encouragement cards for the six weeks I was there. The first week was hard because I did not know much about each team member, but it forced me to really talk with each person so that I had things to write to them and pray for them about.

I could have easily just walked into rehearsal, sang my songs, made pleasant small talk with the band, and called it a day. It would have been easier for me, but do you think that would have been life changing for them? Do you think being casually friendly for six weeks would create a relationship that, years later, would have those team members texting me and staying in contact?

Probably not. There is something about putting forth such effort and exerting such intentionality into relationships that builds strong bonds with people…and I was only with these people for a few weeks. Imagine what it would look like for you if you did this for months with your team. I've done this for years at my home church and even after years of doing it, it doesn't get old. People don't get tired of affirmation! But you don't have to commit to doing it forever. Just commit to trying this for four months and see what happens!

Yeah, it is going to take a good 5-10 minutes for each person, especially since you are not writing the same thing to each person. Each card must be special and unique to each individual, as well as handwritten. If you have a large team like myself, you are potentially looking at having to set aside one to two hours a week to write these 3x5 cards of encouragement. It's going to take time, it's going to take effort, but the exponential growth in relationships it will yield is far worth your efforts!

I know it sounds like a lot of work, and yes it would be easier to just email them or write the same vague thing that applies to each of them, but it loses its value if you do either of those things. Taking the time to write unique cards to each member shows you value them, because you gave what is most valuable of yours to do it…your time. It will become just another reason why you will be the kind of leader followers fight to follow. It is your responsibility as a leader to tangibly love your team.

What Writing an Encouragement Card Does

1. It shows you intentionally set time aside for them. As opposed to just speaking encouragement over them, a card communicates you thought about them beforehand. It wasn't something you just thought of doing, it was something that was calculated, planned, and thus, of more value to them.

2. It keeps you accountable to actually pray for each team member. We can all get caught up in the trap of saying we will pray for someone, but life gets busy, and often prayer is the first thing to go. Writing a weekly card (and including what you have specifically been praying for them about) forces you to actually pray for them. The prayer card, while extremely encouraging to them, also becomes a built-in way to ensure a learned discipline for you as a leader.

3. It gives you the opportunity to show you listen. In your encouragement cards, you can say things like, "I am praying for your grandma's surgery next week," or "for the big exam you have been cramming for," etc. These 3x5s are your chance to show them you actually listen and pay attention to them and their lives outside of worship—that you value them as a person! By giving them a glimpse into your prayers for them, they begin to see how you pray for their whole lives, not just that they would be on time and nail their parts!

4. You will begin to see team members differently. Musicians are a strange breed of people, and a people that can sometimes be irritating to work with and frustrating to be in close spaces with. It becomes all too easy to get frustrated with people and then slowly move from loving them and seeing them as unique creatures of God who were designed for a purpose, to people you simply "put up with." By writing these cards on a weekly basis, you are forced to find things to encourage them on. Some member's cards may be harder to write, taking more thought and effort to do, but after time, you will begin to see their good traits more and more as you search for and write about those good traits.

Don't Get Discouraged

You may be wondering where you are going to get all this information to write a 3x5 card for your team members. The next chapter is going to be a good resource for you in regard to how to have conversations that will eventually give you so much information from each team member you will have trouble keeping your weekly encouragement cards short enough to fit on a 3x5! But in the end, when people see you exerting intentional effort and time towards them (through cards or whatever other ways you think of), they will perceive those actions as love, even if you only write a few sentences the first time around. This alone will change your team culture in ways you cannot believe.

Furthermore, do not be discouraged if you do not receive any feedback from them. I remember the first time I did this. I had spent hours that week praying for my team. I came in early with my little cards and was so excited to put them in each member's spot on stage, knowing it would just make them feel so special!

When they walked in, no one said anything! One guy didn't pick his up. The second gave it a three second glance. And the third guy skimmed his and then threw it in his bag. I remember feeling overwhelmingly sad and discouraged. I had spent so much time on those cards. I had rewritten some of them two or three times to word things just right, and felt like they didn't even care.

First, remember you are not doing this for attention or for a Thank You. Gardeners are rarely praised or appreciated for their hard work, no matter how outstanding. Do not let the response of others dictate your actions. You are not doing it for a response. You are doing it because you are called to do it. You are called to serve, so do so joyfully.

Secondly, remember it is entirely possible that the people being served by you simply do not know how to articulate or communicate their thanks to you. After five months, I found out the same guy who read his card and threw the card in his bag week after week had been saving every card I wrote him and reading them in hard times in his life!

I wanted to surprise him by bringing lunch to his work office one day (which I had never seen before) and was literally speechless at what I saw on his wall. After the secretary buzzed me in, I walked into his office and saw a relatively bare wall. The only things he had pinned up in his entire office was a crayon picture his daughter had drawn him and a string of eight of the 3x5 cards I had written him above his computer. Everything else was white walls.

This whole time I thought he never read a word I wrote, come to find out they were some of the only words of encouragement he had ever received...IN HIS LIFE! You have no idea the power of a 3x5 card.

You never know how your actions affect others, so you give your all, every time, regardless of how they receive it. You have no idea what people are going through; everyone is going through something. You have no idea what that simple card will do for someone. Write to them as if it was the last words of encouragement you could ever share with them, every week.

4 ONE-ON-ONES

Her name was Lily. She was my first crush. I was in 6th grade, and while Taylor Swift was not yet on the scene, I know my love for Lily was the fuel that ignited and sparked every single love song Taylor Swift ever wrote. It was the kind of love that epic novels are written about and passed on throughout the generations.

There was just one small problem; Lily didn't know I existed. I had never worked up the nerve to talk to this angelic woman...until our English teacher Ms. Greene decided to assign a group project.

And guess who ended up in my group? Well, not Lily. No, it took a lot of lunch box trades and video game bribes to weasel my way into a group project with the love of my little 6th grade life, but after many elaborate three to five way trades with my fellow students, I made it happen. But after many recesses of arduous trades to work my way into this small group with Lily, I was met with disappointment.

I was expecting that by the end of the project we

would be best friends and that she just wouldn't be able to resist this hunk of testosterone, but what I found was this: while we had somewhat of a relationship because of shared space and experiences, we still didn't really know each other.

To *really* know someone, you must know more than their favorite color, what kind of car they drive, or other trivial facts about their life. Those are the kinds of things stalkers can find out about you from your social media. Those are the things acquaintances know…it's very surface level. To truly be relational with someone, to truly know them, you should know three things:

1. What that person loves.
2. What that person fears.
3. What that person has lost.

Now I know what you're thinking: I thought this was a book to help me learn how to be a better worship leader, not dating advice from a 6th grader. You're right (that comes at no extra charge…you're welcome:) But this principle for getting to know people goes for anyone in any relationship, *romantic and platonic alike*!

Similar to how I could not truly get to know Lily on a deeper level in the work group atmosphere, you are going to have a very difficult time building deep relationships with your team members if you only spend time with them in the work place (aka during practice and services). You cannot have the quality conversations that lead to the knowledge of those three questions above while you are rehearsing songs, because if you try, it will only distract you from the task at hand—rehearsing to lead the congregation in quality worship that Sunday!

You need to be intentional about making time specifically for these conversations or one-on-ones. *A one-on-one consists of time you set aside specifically to check in, talk with, and share space with one other person, one at a time.*

Why Make Time For A One-On-One

You probably see your team every week, so why take time to meet with them individually outside of rehearsal? You are busy, they are busy, and if you're being honest, you don't even like some of the people on your team! All the more reason a one-on-one is essential to the culture of your team dynamic. Your job as a worship leader is more than just creating pretty music for the congregation. The Lord has entrusted you with the task of loving and leading your team members in life just as much as he expects you to lead your congregation in worship.

The keyboard player to your right is not just a keyboard player. She is also someone's mother, someone's daughter, someone's wife, and someone's best friend. That keyboardist has a past, a story, and a journey that is unique to her. She has struggles, hopes, and fears like anyone else. To only view her as a keyboard player is a mistake. You have an opportunity to invest in her life and to walk alongside her on the journey she has found herself on.

So often we try to get meetings and lunches with the popular people, with the head pastors, with the worship leaders of other churches, and people with whom we have fun, but consider this question: *Do you really think God placed you where you are to surround yourself with the 'cool kids', or to love on those He has already directly surrounded you with?*

Trust that the people in your life have been placed there for a reason, invest and love on them with everything you have and stop squandering your energy on trying to only meet with people who are fun for you. Your team members have been placed in your life, by a God who knows what is best for you and them, for you to encourage and love them and for you to be blessed by them—don't miss this beautiful opportunity you have!

There was a very famous person that was passing through our university and I got to open for him (let's call this person Mr. Teel). I remember I wanted so badly to get a meal with Mr. Teel after the service and was calling in every favor I could think of trying to "accidentally run into" Mr. Teel after service so I could ask him to lunch. I almost became borderline obsessive about getting to hang out with this individual.

I never got the chance to share space with him on a very personal level that day, and with all my obsessing, I almost missed an opportunity that forever changed a relationship I now have with a fellow teammate. As I was leaving the worship center, feeling defeated and discouraged, I happened to pass by my bass player (whom I did not know too well at the time). Since I had no other meetings scheduled for the hour (thinking I would surely be at the lunch of my life by now), I thought I would ask the bass player Casey out to sushi with me.

We ended up talking for almost three hours. It turns out his grandfather had been going through cancer and he had been driving out of town three or four nights a week to take care of him. He would leave our rehearsals to look after his grandfather so his grandmother could run errands.

While I was out goofing off after Sunday services, he would leave the same sanctuary to go feed his grandfather lunch. He sacrificed money in gas, helped pay his grandfather's bills, and gave up a good portion of his social life to take care of this man…and all this time I never saw Casey as anything more than a bass player.

It was over lunch with Casey that afternoon that I realized something: every person I come into contact with has a story. After that conversation, our friendship changed. We were no longer just co-workers. With a single one-on-one, I learned more about Casey than I had after two years of serving with him on a weekly basis. In our brief lunch, a brotherhood was formed. Every interaction that we had following that lunch changed, they were never same. They were richer, deeper, and more meaningful.

Do not overlook your worship team members as people and just see musicians who help you accomplish your own personal goal of pulling off another worship service. People can tell when they are only as valuable as what they can do for you, which models selfishness from the top down. That is not the culture you want to create in your worship family. You want people who work with you and for you to know you see them as people, not potential for your own agenda.

How do you do this? You make time for one-on-ones, and get to know them as individuals. It can sound scary at first to sit down with someone in a one-on-one setting, but the potential benefits far outweigh any potential awkwardness. In the end, you will be grateful you put your efforts toward those who immediately surround you (i.e., your worship team members) and not foolishly wasted valuable time trying to pursue lunch with a famous person and potentially miss out on conversations and defining moments like the one I had with Casey that afternoon.

The funny thing is, a year later I ended up crossing paths with the famous Mr. Teel and got the lunch I had previously so badly desired. The hour we spent at lunch together was fun enough. He said some kind words and told me some amazing stories, but the hour passed and he had another meeting he had to dash off to.

While our lunch was fun for bragging rights, that's about all the lunch was worth. Rubbing shoulders with powerful people is nice for networking reasons and for name-dropping rights at dinner parties, but when real life hits, when trials come and you need a friend at 3 a.m., the Mr. Teel's of your life simply do not have the time or the means to be there for you. The Casey's of your life will.

This is not a criticism of important or high profile people in any way. That just comes with their territory of everyone wanting a piece of their time and often they can only do the big things that they do BECAUSE they don't meet with every person that calls them! It is simply a reminder not to throw away your precious time and energy trying to finagle your way into the lives of the high profile.

Invest in the people who immediately surround you, which more times than not won't be the mayors, the millionaires, or the mighty. If they do naturally end up in your path, love them like you would anybody else. If not, don't envy their time. Just see those who directly surround you as a divine appointment. Cherish every person who organically crosses your path. Be intentional about investing in them on a daily basis.

How To Do A One-On-One

These one-on-ones are not your chance to brag, talk about your importance, who you've rubbed shoulders with, or show off your vast musical knowledge. In fact, these one-on-ones aren't even about you! **Your sole objective during a one-on-one is to make the person you are meeting with feel like the most important person in the world!**

This meeting is not a time for you to ask anything of them, to try and change anything musical they do, or for constructive criticism. There is a time and place for all of those things—this meeting is not it. This meeting is about encouraging them and learning how to love them in whatever way will be most meaningful to them.

Here is something that may help you as you mentally prep for your one-on-one. Imagine you just booked a coffee with whoever your favorite musician or movie star is. How would you interact with them? Would you be on your phone, or would you be hanging on their every word? Would you show up late or would you get there early and go out of your way to meet at places that were convenient for them, even if it's inconvenient for you?

Get a picture of your hero in your head and imagine how you would interact with them before every one-on-one you go into—then make the conscious decision to treat your team member in this same way. It will get you in the correct frame of mind before all your meetings (especially when it is with someone you do not particularly look forward to meeting with!).

Over the years, I have also found the following suggestions to work extremely well for myself and have seen others have great success as they implement them into their one-on-ones with their worship teams.

1. Learn to say, "It's on me."

At the very start of the meeting, before you begin any conversation, set the foundation that *you are for them* by treating them. If you go to coffee, buy their coffee. If you go to sushi, buy their sushi. Regardless of if you have an expense account or this is coming out of your own pocket, find a way to treat them.

Chances are they freely volunteer hours and hours of their time, week after week. The least you can do is communicate you value and honor them by treating them to a coffee or a meal. Fight them for the bill if you have to—bite, claw, scratch—do what you need to do, but you pick up their tab!

Do not be stingy with what the Lord has given you! Be known as a leader of remarkable generosity. It is small actions like this which, over time, win your team members over and invoke a desire to follow you into battle! It is so rare to be treated to anything with no strings attached these days that this simple action will set your relationship and meeting time with them above the rest!

Remember, your time of meeting with them is not to ask for anything, correct anything, or criticize them in any way. Your sole purpose is to make them feel like the most valued and important person in the room. You start by treating them, and ask nothing in return.

2. Shut Your Mouth and Listen

More times than not, your team members are not

looking for answers, or your advice (though I am sure you have just the best advice in the world, and if everyone listened to you, the world would be a better place).

People just want to feel heard. You may have the answers…awesome. Save that for the last 10 minutes of your hour meeting. Again, this meeting time is not for you to show off all your biblical knowledge and great wisdom, it is a time for you to listen, empathize, laugh, and let them be the star of the conversation.

All too often we let others talk for a minute, then follow up their story saying, "That's funny… it reminds me of a time when I…" We hijack the conversation, putting the attention and spotlight back on us. Most of the time we aren't even listening to what the other person is saying—we listen for what we can add to the conversation.

Think about it, Joe Shmoe starts talking about his favorite worship leading experience, and that sets your mind off to your own favorite worship leading experience. Then while the person is finishing their thought, you are thinking about how you are going to respond to them and tell your own story, then you end up not listening and just prepping your own response.

It is how we have been trained to communicate, but just because it is the norm in our culture does not mean it is the best way to communicate with others. It takes intentionality and awareness to break this habit. Learning to push aside your self-centered thought patterns and tendency to shift the attention of the conversation back on yourself is one of the most loving things you can do for another in conversation.

The first 50 minutes you should only be asking open-ended

questions, and actively listening. That is how you make people feel valued and how you grow as a leader. Besides, who knows what you might learn if you learn to shut your mouth and assume a humble position of teachability!

3. Learn the Art of Asking Questions

Questions in conversation display humility—it shifts the focus off of you and back onto the other person. Questions demonstrate an interest in the other person. They invite others into the dance of dialogue. They can guide, redirect, and deepen the course of the conversation. The ability and willingness to ask questions separates those who are effective conversationalists and those who are not.

But have you ever stopped to think that there are different types of questions? In my training and travels, I find that not many people know there are different types of questions, and that different types of questions do different types of things. Below are a list of question types and what they will do for you and your conversations.

Closed Questions. The death of a conversation comes from closed questions, which only require a one word answer. For example, if you ask someone, "Are you going to the store?" they can answer in one word, yes or no. If you only ask closed questions your conversations will suffer greatly—what you need are open-ended questions.

Open-Ended Questions. Open-ended questions are the *What, Why, and How* kinds of questions that ask for much more developed responses than a closed question.

For example, you can turn the same question above

into an open-ended question that births rich conversation and draws out more information from the person you are talking with by adding one word: Why. *"WHY are you going to the store?"*

Do you see how that one word completely changes the potential of the conversation? The potential that lies in an open-ended question, and its ability to stimulate more developed answers from others is one of the most powerful skills you possess. Open-ended questions will enable you to get the other person to open up more than any other single conversational skill.

Probing Questions. Probing questions are specific questions that are directly related to the information you receive from the person you are talking to. Probing questions ask for additional information that helps the person you are talking to further explain, describe, and develop their ideas, thoughts, and feelings.

These types of questions help to encourage people to expand their thinking, and really explore and seek out the meaning behind the words. The use of probing questions will actually help the speaker discover more about him or herself.

Observe how Tyler uses probing questions to help Molly, the worship leader of a small church, explore her thoughts and feelings:

Tyler: "Hey Molly! How are you doing?" (open)
Molly: "I'm okay."
Tyler: "**How** is worship going at your church?"(open & probing)

Molly: "I wish I didn't even work here anymore!"

Tyler: "**Why**?" (probing)

Molly: "Well, I just thought I would be more successful by now!"

Tyler: "**What** do you mean by 'successful'?" (open & probing)

Molly: "I just thought my church would be bigger by now!"

Tyler: "The numbers might not be what you wanted, but **how** are the people who are there growing spiritually?" (open & probing)

Molly: "Well, I guess the few people we have are really learning how to worship freely and are excited about it!"

Tyler: "That's great! **How** does that make you feel?" (open & probing)

Molly: "It really encourages me, actually. I remember the first time I saw people start to understand freedom in worship, and it made me so happy to see!"

Tyler: "**What** other things has the Lord been doing?" (open & probing)

Molly: You know, he has been so faithful in providing people, musicians, and tech support that have lifted such a burden from my shoulders these last few months!"

Tyler: "I think the Lord's really blessing your efforts, Molly!"

Molly: "Hey, thanks for the talk Tyler, I appreciate it!"

Tyler: "My pleasure!"

Did you notice how Tyler's six probing questions encouraged Molly to talk, explore, and eventually draw a different conclusion on the success of her ministry at church? Did you see how Tyler *didn't judge, evaluate, or give advice,* but simply asked for additional information with his probing questions?

These are the types of questions you want to begin incorporating into your meetings (and everyday conversations) as they will take your conversations and relationships to depths never explored before. These questions are the single most important tool you can learn to use to become the best leader you can be.

Another rule of thumb for any Gardener is this: Be more concerned with being <u>interested</u> than <u>interesting</u>. If you can master this rule, people will flock to you and love you as a leader! Chances are they are already impressed with you, no need to talk more about yourself. What they really want is to be heard, because to be listened to and heard is to be loved.

4. Smile

I know this sounds like a simple thing, but being able to smile while listening to another can make all the difference in the world. Often I do not think we realize how stern we look as we try to listen attentively. It can be intimidating to try and open up to someone who is staring at you without a smile! So don't be emo, flash that pretty little smile! And laugh easily and heartily!

Who doesn't like someone who laughs easily with you? Everyone likes to feel funny, even when they aren't explicitly trying to be humorous. It will help them to feel comfortable and boost their confidence in the conversation.

5. Speak Life

When you make it to the last 15% of your time together, after you have sat and listened and let them talk (only interjecting to ask questions), it is finally your turn to talk, BUT REMEMBER this is not a time to shift the focus onto yourself and share all the hilarious stories and antidotes you've been holding back and secretly thinking about while they talked...no. This meeting is still all about them.

Now is the time you get to speak, but your conversation with them should start like this..."I loved when you said _____." This first off shows you were listening to them and also that you remembered what they said (active listening!). Once you pave the way with mirroring a few things they shared, you can now encourage them. This is your chance to speak life into them, to share what you are seeing the Lord do in and through them, and build them up!

6. Take Notes

No, not in the meeting...that's weird and makes your casual get-togethers feel far too formal. You are going to have to mentally retain all the information they talked about in that hour until they walk out of the coffee shop or until you get back to your office or your home. Once you are back home, keep a folder or a word document or a notes tab on your phone where you can jot down a few notes on what that person shared that you might forget (e.g., his mother is ill, her sister is moving to Nebraska, your guitarist is struggling with loneliness, etc.).

It sounds silly, but chances are, the bigger your

operation gets, the more and more meetings you will have, and some of these little details may slip through the cracks. If you can take a minute or two to jot down some notes, you can review them before your next meeting or look at it as you pray for them and write their 3x5 encouragement cards! Don't assume you will remember everything. Take time to write it down.

Implementation: The Six Steps

If you begin to put these six suggestions into practice (Learn to say, "It's on me," Shut your mouth and listen, Learn the art of asking questions, Smile, Speak life, and Take notes), your one-on-ones with people will begin to visibly change, offering amazing opportunities for growth and change.

You will find people enjoy and look forward to meeting with you, primarily because everyone likes to be treated to things, to talk, to feel funny, to be encouraged, and to be remembered; and few people give them the space to do or have these things. When they find someone like you who creates a safe atmosphere for them to explore their thoughts and they are the center of attention for the whole conversation, you will find them wanting to meet weekly!

I had one leader who incorporated these things into our weekly meetings with me when I started working at the university. At first, I didn't want another person on my calendar or another meeting to attend. I was already so busy! But after my second lunch meeting at Chick-fil-A with Daniel, who implemented all of these techniques, I was finding that those one-on-one meetings with him were one of the few things I really looked forward to in my weekly calendar. Out of all the people and things that were a drain on me, Daniel (and Chick-fil-A) were life giving.

Don't misunderstand me, incorporating these six things into your meetings will not be easy. They even have the potential to leave you feeling discouraged, lonely, and frustrated at times. I have left many meetings where I poured ridiculous amounts of energy into loving and listening to the other person, only to walk away flustered that they didn't ask ME one question.

But those frustrations are my flesh. Remember you are there for them; ask nothing in return. You are not doing these things for reciprocation, you are doing it out of love for your team members. *The gardener philosophy of leadership does not call us to easy, it calls us to excellence.* These meetings will be hard at times, but trust it is well worth your investments!

Section 3
Creating the Ideal Congregation

5 FIRST THINGS FIRST

You are up there leading worship, giving it 110% in every song in every service, pouring your blood, sweat, and tears into every lick of every note you play—only to look out week after week to see people standing with their hands in their pockets, looking down at their phone, or straight up ignoring you and talking to their neighbor.

This happened to me many times, and I can remember feeling beyond frustrated. One time in particular I had my eyes closed, and thought we had really tapped into something special in worship, only to open my eyes to see people staring blankly back at me. I had the urge to walk out into the audience and SHAKE people, asking, DON'T YOU FEEL THE SPIRIT HERE?! What in the world is wrong? Why are you consistently disengaged?!

There are many different solutions to help remedy the congregational apathy that seems to plague so many churches, but before we look at any of those things, we need to look at the foundational "first things first."

First Things First

Yes, you can create a good culture apart from the Holy Spirit; it can even be a great culture. In fact, I once went to a Coldplay concert, and it was emotionally moving. If I didn't know better, I would have said it was a spiritual experience. The lights were going, the music was perfect, and I was caught up in mass hysteria. The world creates amazing cultures and atmospheres all the time because they have learned specific skillsets and "tricks of the trade" that help move them further faster.

But think about this: **if people without the power of the Living God can create an encouraging, life-giving atmosphere, how much better should ours be?** We have access to all the same information and knowledge they do, PLUS we have the power that raised Christ from the dead working within us and in our services! Our gatherings should be blowing people out of the water, week after week.

We are going to look at a lot of practical tools on creating an ideal congregational culture, and there is nothing wrong with utilizing these "tricks of the trade," but these things are only meant to enhance our services. We should not rely on any one of these things for our church's success.

The first things first: "Unless the Lord builds the house, the builders labor in vain. Unless the Lord watches over the city, the guards stand watch in vain. In vain you rise early and stay up late, toiling for food to eat…" (Psalm 127:1-2).

We are called to faithfulness, not just fruitfulness. The reality is you are not responsible for changing the heart of any person in your congregation. That "fruit" is the

Lord's job and comes from your faithfulness. Your job is to be faithful to do everything the Lord has called you to do and after you have put in all the work you can, leave the results up to God. It's not a cop out for you to be lazy, but should lift a lot of unnecessary anxiety off of your shoulders.

In the story of the Talents that Jesus shares in Matthew 25, the good servant who invests his money is rewarded not for the *fruit* (or return) of his investments, but for his *faithfulness* to the process of what God called him to do. Jesus did not say, "Well done, good and *fruitful* servant," did he? No. Jesus says, "Well done, good and FAITHFUL servant" (Matthew 25:23). This is a good thing to remember and the foundation we need to start from.

The first things first: in and of your own power you can do nothing. Stop relying on yourself and dedicate yourself to the pursuit of faithfulness, not just fruitfulness. Do everything *you* possibly can, then rest easy knowing you were faithful to the process and let the Holy Spirit do His job.

The Process

So we have the first thing in its rightful first place— we are chasing after faithfulness— but what are we being faithful to doing? Amazing question, I am glad you asked. After reading the first two sections of this book, you are already on the path to success with personal and worship team dynamics. Keep faithful to those things discussed in the first two sections and maintain continual upkeep on them (this is no "one and done" kind of thing) but we are now ready to move on to the next section. The next step is getting people offstage (aka the congregation) to follow you. To begin, know this: *if people don't follow you offstage, they won't follow you onstage.*

I few years back I was asked to fill in for a guitarist at the church of a worship leader whom I was particularly fond of. I had never met this person but had always enjoyed his music and was looking forward to playing with him! We never talked during rehearsal, but after one of the main sessions I ended up running into this artist in the bathroom of all places and as we were leaving I tried to spark up a conversation and ask him how his day was.

I can vividly remember him making eye contact, grunting something about not having time to talk, and walking away. I was shocked. This man who I had listened to for years was a jerk...a JERK! I was convinced of it! For the next year I couldn't listen to his music the same way, knowing that in real life he was not a nice man...probably not even a Christian, (well, that's what my 16 year old self decided anyway!)

Now in reality, he was probably having a bad day, or I misunderstood him, or he really was in a hurry and was heartbroken about our short exchange as he thought back on it later that evening. But as a young high schooler, all I knew was that offstage I didn't like him, and because of that one encounter, I could never listen to him onstage the same way.

Was that fair of me? No. Do people do this to you with every interaction they have with you? Yes.

Every interaction we have with people either enlarges or diminishes the opportunity to build rapport with them.

In every interaction you have, you are creating for the other person a filter through which they see you. The more positive that filter is offstage, the more positively it will be amplified when they see you onstage.

When I was in junior high, David Crowder was my hero. I had every album of his, I knew every song by heart, and I had pictures of him as my screen saver...I was man-crushing on Crowder hard core. When I was in 7th grade, I attended a big festival called Spirit West Coast, mostly because I heard Crowder was going to be performing there!

It was the evening that he was performing and I simply could not wait to see him live! I used the outhouses before the concert started, but as I was walking in, I thought I saw a tall, skinny bearded figure walking out of the one next to me. I thought, surely Crowder doesn't use the OUTHOUSES like us common folk! But just in case, I followed this giant of a man...and sure enough, it was CROWDER!

And he was so kind. He was on his way to walk onstage but stopped everything to talk to one fan. A nobody. A 7th grade kid. He posed for a picture, asked questions about my life, and spent some quality time talking with me, and was even a few minutes late to perform to thousands because he took time to invest in just a random kid who loved him and what he did. That single interaction changed how I saw him, heard his music, and forever talked about him when his name came up in conversation.

So whether you're standing in line after service to get coffee, or walking out to your car and happen to walk by a congregation member, *initiate conversation*! Every opportunity you have, whether it's a quick hello, or it ends up being a 15 minute conversation, make every person you pass feel more important and loved than before they shared space with you. And while you can't always talk and meet with every person in the congregation, if you are nice to everyone you DO pass by, your reputation as being friendly and nice will precede you throughout the whole church.

Don't pick and choose who you say hi to or who you greet; make your motto: if it breathes, I'll greet it. No matter how big or small your church is, this is important. I grew up in a church of 100 people, and now serve at a church of over 12,000. It is important at both and equally possible at any size church.

You are not too busy or too important to greet people as you walk around and that single action may very well change how people perceive you onstage for the rest of their time at your church! Not to mention you will begin to set a culture at your church from the top down of friendliness.

Learn To Want What You Already Have

According to the U.S. Congregational Life Survey (USCLS), 59% of the churches in America are comprised of 7-99 members, and 35% of churches in America are comprised of 100-499 members. That means that 94% of all churches in the United States have less than 500 people in their services. I happened to grow up in that first 59 percentile.

My first church was a small family church. Everyone knew everyone, and I loved it. But somewhere in my early teens I discovered YouTube and was opened up to the allures of Hillsong and Passion Conferences and got to see mega churches. I must confess, in my youth, the desires of my heart shifted to wanting to play on massive stages like my heroes did! I would spend less and less time at the church where the Lord currently had me and would instead daydream about the day I could move on to "real ministry" and play with the big boys.

If I have one regret of my early ministry years, it was all the time and energy I wasted envying those with bigger stages than me. With a heavy heart, I look back on all the missed opportunities I passed up and all the relationships I neglected in the church RIGHT WHERE I WAS because I was too preoccupied with envying where I could be.

We often have a tendency to go towards THE BIG things. This is something you have to get over because it will drain you of faithfulness to where you are currently planted and will cause you to overlook the people that the Lord has currently surrounded you with. Remain faithful to the process. Remain faithful to where God currently has you planted. If he moves you somewhere bigger, great. Be faithful there. If he keeps you where you are currently planted forever, great. Be faithful there. Be faithful.

6 BEING INCARNATIONAL
(Pre-Service Prayer)

As a freshman in college, I attended weekly chapels with hundreds of my fellow students. I was not in the "worship crowd." I knew none of them and none of them knew me. I just sat back and envied them with all that was in me. Like so many other freshmen at this Christian university, I was a big shot worship leader for the youth at my old church back home, only to come to a school where no one knew or respected me. I had no name or status in the worship world here like I did just a few short months ago before I moved into this new college community.

Every Wednesday and Friday mornings, I would find my seat for chapel and watch as the worship team gathered backstage with the guest speaker the university had flown in for that chapel and they would talk over the service and pray together. I can remember how much I wished I could be one of those members…they were so cool! They were backstage, they got to rub shoulders with all the famous speakers who came through, and here I was, a nobody, just sitting in my seat waiting for them to finish their pre-service rituals and take the stage so the service could begin and we could all begin worship.

By the time my sophomore year rolled around, I had been given some opportunities to lead and proven myself in the worship scene at the university and was now a part of the worship team that I envied so much the year before. I finally got to go backstage and talk and pray with speakers and walk the path lined with neon green tape to the stairs that led to the brightly lit stage…

But what I found was this…the hearts of the "backstage group" were sincere. They were faithfully praying for those in the congregation. Their prayers and desire for their worship experience were heartfelt and honest. I had thought they were just trying to be cool standing around backstage and taking special paths to the stage, but once I was given the opportunity to be around it, I saw their hearts were humble, and things like the walkway to the stage were not a pride trip for most of the musicians, it was just the most time effective and efficient way to get to the stage.

It was this experience that led me to a very important realization that changed my actions as a leader: **perception is reality to the receiver.** How the person receiving any kind of information perceives it, in turn, makes up how they view reality. Reality is in the eye of the beholder.

Were the musicians trying to be rock stars and invoke envy? No. But how were their actions being perceived? While they were doing nothing wrong and had pure hearts, it was being perceived by the congregation as arrogance and an "us and them" segregation between the cool worship team and the common lay people.

This is important: it doesn't matter how pure your heart is or how humble you are…if your actions are being perceived as arrogant or a form of class hierarchy, they WILL affect how people see you, your ministry, and ultimately how they enter into worship.

If they think you want to be a rock star, then you get onstage and lead passionately from a place of humility, some may think you are faking it or that your humility is just an act. This will be cause for distraction to them during worship. How the receiver decodes your actions will in turn result in their perception of reality.

My following junior year I was given the role of University Worship Coordinator. One of the primary things I worked on was helping people in the congregation get an accurate perception of the true humility of the worship team's heart. One of the ways I did this was by becoming incarnational.

The idea of becoming incarnational in your ministry is to fully immerse yourself in the culture which you are trying to affect, finding common ground and ways to be like the people you are trying to reach. Similar to how Jesus became a man incarnate to get on our level, we too are to be incarnational and find ways to become like the people we are trying to reach. The primary way I trained leaders to become incarnational to the non-worship team group (i.e., the congregation) is through a revised pre-service prayer.

Pre-Service Prayer

Having been on the outside of the green room, or on "the other side of the curtain" as I liked to say (since our greenroom was just behind a big black curtain that divided the stage and the people…) I knew perception equaled reality, and for the other people's perception or "reality" sake, we needed to change how we did pre-service prayer.

Rather than hide backstage and have a group of eight leaders pray for the people they were about to lead in worship, I wanted them to GO OUT into the congregation and be incarnational with (or become like) those they wanted to affect and lead. I would send those eight team members OUT individually into the congregation to find people that arrived early (often sitting on their phones or looking at a bulletin) and have them each form groups of five or six around them and ask those people to pray WITH them.

This did a number of things that greatly changed our whole congregational church culture…

1. Mix With the People

Rather than just the "super cool, holy worship team" clique hiding behind the curtain, it gets us off our proverbial pedestal and helps to alleviate any unspoken culture of "us and them" and reminds the people we are no more holy and no more special because we are on a stage. Our prayers are no more special or exceptional than theirs.

2. Multiply

Instead of eight leaders praying over a service and the congregation sitting in their seats waiting for the worship to begin, you send those eight individuals out to rally groups of five or six congregation members, and now you have eight small groups (or FORTY to FORTY-EIGHT people) praying over the service! More people praying is always a good thing!

3. Disciple Through Action

Instead of praying that people would enter your church doors with a spirit of expectancy and a heart ready to worship (which is rather passive), you take action to help create that kind of culture. You go out and train them in what to pray for and things to say, then by the time worship starts, they are already in a state of mind to worship. It is you and your team DISCIPLING your congregation in how to worship in ways beyond just singing songs.

This also means no more "first song, throw away song." I used to start worship with a "throw away song" because I knew people weren't going to worship in those first four minutes of my sets—it was really just to get everyone's attention and get them to stop talking. But when half your congregation is praying over the service (and not chatting, or playing on their phones, etc.) the culture of the room shifts, and all those who enter feel something different.

4. Build Community

It builds community. When I go out, I usually look for a few small groups of two or three, introduce myself and have everyone meet each other, then we pray together. It forces people to get out of their comfort zone and meet new people, and you act as a bridge to their relationship.

Changing Culture

I used to walk out on stage from behind the curtain and look out to see people distracted and I would feel the need to start the service with a joke or a funny anecdote to draw them in, then struggled the entire worship set to get them to a place of spirit-filled, truthful worship. Now, after a few months of sending my team and myself out to pray with people pre-service, I walk out onstage and look out to a sea of small groups, huddled up in prayer asking God to show up and do amazing things for his name's sake.

The end result is amazing, but I'm not going to lie to you…*changing culture is always hard. People don't like different.* So if they are used to coming to church and sitting and not being bothered, you and your team going out and asking people to pray with them has the potential to be very difficult or uncomfortable.

I am an introvert. I don't like feeling uncomfortable or talking with strangers when I do not have to. But here's the deal: *the potential ramifications of this small act could change the entire culture and heartbeat of your church. Isn't that potential culture change of a church well worth feeling a little uncomfortable for two minutes for the first three or four weeks you do this?*

Now that sounds nice in theory, but if you are anything like me, you may be trying to talk yourself out of more work by saying things like, "But I'm tired. I just want to sit in the green room and eat donuts with my friends. After all, I have to play at SIX services, don't I deserve some rest time in between services? How can I serve others if I'm not taking care of myself?"

More times than not, these are just excuses. If you're tired, go to bed earlier. If you're still tired, maybe you need to take some time off before you burn out. And you don't need that extra donut anyway, you know you're still trying to drop that weight you gained at Thanksgiving this year! You have plenty of other times to take care of yourself. These few hours you are serving at the weekend services is not only your responsibility to invest in the culture of the church, it is also more than likely part of your paid occupation to do so!

If you STILL need more persuasion, I recommend this in all sincerity…visit a different church. Take a weekend off, find a random church where you know NO ONE and attend a service or two there. Be an outsider again. Remember what it feels like to be new and to NOT know everyone in the church. Embrace the feeling of awkwardness and loneliness. *Sometimes it takes being an outsider to be reminded of the importance of inclusivity and friendliness.*

Offstage Worship

The second big change we implemented in an attempt to be more incarnational was something I like to call an "offstage acoustic" set. It's pretty much all in its name. Every two or three months we like to have a worship set that symbolically represents what our hearts always are. We like to symbolically represent that worship is always, was always, and will forever be centered around the glory of the triune Godhead.

The way we symbolically represent this is by moving all our musicians and instruments offstage (on the ground where no one can really see us) and clearing the stage of everything except one cross that we put front and center. It is a great visual reminder for the congregation that worship is not about a particular band, or a person, or a fancy stage design, but about the cross and Christ crucified. It's all they look at, thus what their minds focus on!

The reason we do not do this every week is because we believe that electric guitars, intricate instrumentation and a good looking stage can all ADD to a worship experience, but a few times a year we remove all of it to ensure that we can still worship without them (i.e., that we are not worshiping those things!) and to remind us that those things do not make a worship service powerful, the Holy Spirit does. They are simply tools that the Father has gifted us with to enhance our experience.

Seek the Lowly and Lonely

Lastly, as you consider how to be incarnational in your job and as a leader and decide you are going to come out from behind the curtain and talk with people in the congregation, there will be a temptation to seek out the most powerful business men in your church, or see it as an opportunity to network with that extremely wealthy individual. So as you decide to become incarnational, heed this instruction: *do not leverage your position of influence to surround yourself with the elite. Find the proverbial 'lepers' (or neglected) of the group and invest in them.*

I mean honestly, as you see the example set before us by Jesus, do you really think the Lord placed you where you are to surround yourself with the cool kids? Or perhaps did he give you this platform so that you might have more opportunity to give attention and love to those who have possibly never received it before?

I must warn you though, no matter how much energy you put out in your pre-service prayer time, no matter how many people you invest in or how hard you try to have a good name among God and men, there will still be those who dislike you for (seemingly) no reason. The next chapter addresses how to deal with these types of people.

7 DISARMING THE HATERS

We have all felt the pressures and stresses of a visible leadership position. You take coffee date after coffee date and still someone is not happy or still feels neglected. You try to do more hymns, and the young people are upset; you do more current, upbeat hits and the older generation complains.

No matter what you do, someone is yelling at you, someone is writing you angry emails, and you're on the brink of burn out trying to be "all things to all people." You begin to feel suffocated by the opinions, desires, and (often unfair) standards people place on you. The weight is excruciating.

Let me start by first saying, you are not alone. This is not a battle unique to you and your church culture, this happens in every organization, to every leader, both in and out of the church world. Not only are you not alone, but you are not necessarily doing anything wrong either just because people are angry. Here is a rule that I realized at an early age that gave me an enormous amount of freedom (and I hope it does the same for you!) Let me introduce you to the 10-80-10 Rule.

The 10-80-10 Rule

The 10-80-10 Rule is simple. It is a matter of percentages made of up lovers, haters, and the honest. It is my personal theory that no matter what you do, no matter how amazing or awful of a leader you are, 10% of people will love you no matter what, 10% of people will hate you no matter what, and the other 80% of people's opinions can be swayed based on their interactions with you and your perceived persona and reputation.

The Lovers (10%)

The first 10% of people will love you no matter what you do or who you are. These are people like your spouse, your mother, your father, your children, your grandparents, etc. No matter where you are serving, you will find these people. Sometimes they are family members, other times they are just people who idolize you and honestly believe you can do no wrong.

They are the ones who tell you how great of a job you did even after you miss a majority of your notes, your voice cracks, you trip walking offstage and try to catch your balance on a table of candles knocking wax all over and almost setting the whole church on fire (yeah, cause this totally isn't a true story of mine or anything….)

The Lovers are a 10% that are important to have in your life, and are key to have around to help fill and encourage you. There is nothing wrong with hanging out with these people; however, they are not a reliable source for you to *solely* gauge your effectiveness by. They will let you slide on things and may not see or mention faults that everyone else sees. If you only surround yourself with these people, you will have a very skewed view of reality, and it will make you an ineffective leader in the end. Be aware of who these people are, enjoy them and go to them for encouragement, but do not base your reality solely on what they say.

The Haters (10%)

The next 10% are the haters. Now I realize this is not a common term for people outside of my generation or people who are not up on the current rap music lingo, so for the sake of clarity, let me define what I mean by a "hater." A hater is someone who doesn't like you. My good friends over at Urban Dictionary describe a hater as such: "A person that develops a strong dislike for another, solely basing their own opinion on personal judgment rather than objective merit. The formation of a hater's contempt commonly arises from jealously and/or resentment."

Haters are always going to be there, and "haters always gunna hate." It is most people's natural tendency to do anything to please the haters in hopes that they can get EVERYONE to like them, but you know as well as I do that getting everyone to like you is impossible, thus foolish to try and do.

I was leading a youth conference a while back and a middle-age man ended up finding me while I ate lunch and decided to join me. The rest of that lunch consisted of him telling me how he questioned my salvation and my role as a leader because I had not sung a single hymn (this is after the first main session, for a very contemporary junior high winter retreat that was aimed at unbelievers). But all the same, I was this man's captive audience for almost an hour, and by the end of the hour, I started doubting all my decisions in song selection!

Maybe he was right! Maybe he was a prophet whom the Lord *had* told to correct my sinful ways of not singing hymns! I was so discouraged (and partially assumed if he was this gung-ho about it, it must be the belief held by all) so I changed the night session set list to all hymns…. Needless to say, it went horribly. I believe a glow stick was even thrown at my head by a dissatisfied 7th grade boy at one point.

In my years of experience in leadership and in the church, this is what I learned: it is usually a bad idea to cater to the minority (or if you're looking for a catchy little slogan: "don't *cater* to the *hater*!"). It is foolish to try and change your entire church culture based on this small (but often LOUD) minority. No matter what you do, no matter what you change, the 10% in the hater camp will always stay. If your actions change, the people may change, but they will always be replaced. The 10% stays constant no matter what you do.

Heck, even Jesus had haters! Remember that. Jesus had Pharisees, and people around every turn who wanted him dead. If even Jesus, all-knowing, all-powerful JESUS was unable to make everyone happy, who are you to think YOU can live a life without haters?

We are going to go more in depth about how to deal

with haters later in this chapter (especially when haters start to exceed the 10% that we have allowed them in this 10-80-10 Rule!) so keep that definition in the back of your mind. And if you are older than 30 and had never heard that term before…you're welcome. You are one step closer to making a youthful friend, equipped with the weapon of "hip lingo!"

The Honest (80%)

Lastly we have the most important percentile. We have the 80% who are not dedicated to loving or hating you. We have the *true mirror percentile*. This is the one we as leaders want to pay attention to; these are the people who can be a good indicator of if we are doing our jobs well.

It can be dangerous territory to start judging how you are doing based on the approval of man, but that is not what this *true mirror* percentile is about. It is just one of many effective tools to keep us in touch with reality; and reality is always our friend. It only becomes dangerous when you let what other people think move from being a tool to a dictating force in your life.

While you will always have haters, if they increase past 10% and you start noticing more and more emails are coming in from people saying you are growing arrogant in the way you carry yourself, or that you are being exclusive, etc., to the point that the usual 10% haters are growing to a bigger 30 or 40%, you may want to pay a little more attention.

This 80% gives a relatively objective view of how you are doing at your job. These people that make up the honest 80% are the people who don't initially hate or love you, which makes their stance toward you the best meter to read from (as opposed to the other 10%ers who have strong biases for or against you).

At my university, chapel was mandatory. A lot of students did not want to be there, and a particular group of students got a bad rap for being blatantly obvious about their objection to having to attend chapel. They would sit in the back right section. They would bring laptops, listen to their own music during worship, and lie down and sleep during the messages. It was one of the most discouraging things I have ever encountered.

While the group was primarily made of up athletes, not all of them were athletes and not all the athletes were a part of this problem. That said, the majority of these people in the back right section did sports of some kind, so rather than send staff back there to force them to pay attention and MAKE them engage in chapel, I instructed our team to take a different approach.

We started to involve the athletes who were solid in their faith in our worship services (to sing, or pray, or do announcements) and encourage them to be leaders. This got them to have some buy-in into the chapel experience.

Then, even though they blatantly disrespected us while we were onstage, I got our whole worship team together to attend and cheer on our athletes at a majority of their games. We downloaded rosters, would memorize names of athletes and look over stats so that when we saw them, we could call them by name and encourage them!

Now before your write this off and say, "Well, Jared is a guy, of course he loved going to games and looking at basketball stats…" I have to correct you. I hate sports. I have never watched a full football game (never even the

Super Bowl! I usually just go for the snacks and leave before the first inning is over…football is that sport with innings, right?! RIGHT?!) So this was a sacrifice for me. I had to do things I didn't like to win over the people who were placed under my pastoral care.

We won over a lot of the athletes from that back right row, and if you were to attend a chapel today, you would see the majority of the athletic teams sitting in the front row. No staff pressures or rules implemented, we just went out of our way to win them over, and get part of that 80% into the approval corner.

Haters Gunna Hate, Right?

Now even with all of this effort, there will still be those who dislike you, those who speak against you, and those you just cannot win over. Accepting the fact that you cannot please everyone will save you a great deal of anxiety and should relieve a great burden from your shoulders.

However, there is danger in this revelation. Understanding that everyone will not always like you (and being okay with that) is essential to sustainability in leadership; BUT, it's half a revelation short of a complete, godly outlook on leadership.

While you cannot control other's actions, words, or thoughts towards you, and while you should not carry the burden of responsibility for those things, you are responsible for yourself and your own actions. *Simply put, we cannot use "Haters Gunna Hate" as an excuse to not put effort in our relationships or trying to minimize the number of haters to as few as possible in our lives!*

Romans 12:18 says, "If it is possible, as far as it depends on you, live at peace with everyone!" We are not responsible for people liking us. We ARE responsible for doing everything in our power, in every action and interaction with others, to make sure we are not putting up any additional barriers for them to like us.

With this in mind, how are we supposed to do our part to live at peace with haters while maintaining realistic expectations and understanding not everyone will love us? What did I do with the athletes of my university who sat in that back right corner? What a great question. I am glad you asked. The answer is hidden in an idea that I call "Double Time."

Double Time

Most people have a judgment system for people in their life. They have the people they like, the people they don't, and the people they are indifferent to. For the sake of clarity, let's assign a numerical value to these:

> **RELATIONSHIP SCALE**
> (-10)----(-5)----(0)----(+5)----(+10)
>
> **KEY:**
> (-10) = Someone you want to poke in the eyeball
> (0) = Someone you are indifferent towards
> (+10) = Someone you would take a bullet for

When two strangers meet for the first time, they usually both start at a zero (or an unknowing indifference) and then they begin moving left or right on the scale depending on a series of judgments based on their interactions with the other (i.e., how they speak, what they wear, their sense of humor, their social group, etc.).

The people who are your friends are people who have done things in your life that meant enough for you to move them up from zero into the positive numbers towards a 10. The people you hate in your life are the people who have done something to hurt or offend you in some way, causing you to move them down from zero into the negatives closer to -10 (aka, I want to poke them in the eyeball status...).

But what you have in common with every person in your life is that at some point, they were a stranger. At some point, you didn't know them, and they started at a zero until you did have the first meeting. From that first moment on, you have been categorizing them in your mind as friend or foe, moving them left (-) or right (+) based off of every interaction you have with them. They had a fair start, their status in your life is likely based on their own actions.

But for a worship leader, we are at a disadvantage that we often do not even know about or think about. Many people in the congregation look at the worship leader week after week, and struggle with the disconnect of why YOU are in a position of attention and THEY are not. Because you are on a stage and because many know you, you are envied by many.

You have something that most people want. When you walk onstage, everyone knows you. Everyone knows your name. Everyone recognizes you. Meanwhile, John Doe sits in the audience week after week, only known by a few, only recognized by some. And after a while, John Doe begins to grow insecure as he compares himself to you, and his defense mechanism to his insecurity is to hate you. If he can talk down about you in his mind, he can elevate and feel better about himself.

This puts you at a great disadvantage when you meet John Doe. Unlike most other first meetings, *you* do not initially start at zero with John Doe. He has already categorized you. Before you even meet him, HE has already decided he does not like you. He has prejudged and evaluated you. He has already made up reasons not to like you (your pants are too tight, you must be a hipster, or you haven't said hi to me until now so you must be a pretentious jerk, or I always see you laughing after you get offstage, you probably don't take God seriously, etc.) and has already moved you into the negative side of the scale previously shown above.

This is where the idea of Double Time comes in. While it would usually take "X" amount of effort and intentionality to become friends with a stranger, John Doe has already categorized you in the negatives, so you not only have to put in the normal amount of effort you would with a person to become friends, you also have to put in extra effort just to get out of the negatives and back to the neutral "0" zone! So while it would take anyone else "X" amount of time and energy to befriend John Doe, it takes you "2x," or double time!

Now is this fair to you as a worship leader? Not in the least. But fair or not, I guarantee you will encounter this time and time again, and unless you want your church to be filled with people who would recognize you offstage, but have a bad taste in their mouth when they do see you, you need to know how to deal with this. So what's the solution?

The only remedy for people's envy is to start a relationship with them. *Friendship alleviates the tension of competition.* And the beautiful thing about the John Does of your life is that once you put that effort in to befriend them, they are often the people who are loyal for life!

Maybe it's because all the energy they used to obsess over and direct towards hating you has to shift somewhere when you decided to befriend them, or maybe it's just a personality type, but *once you befriend them, your loudest haters will become your biggest advocates.* Suddenly, your wins become their wins. Once you've won them over to your camp, they are amazing people to have in your congregation and you will be grateful for them (that's right, that person that has been in your head the whole time you've been reading this section...you will be grateful for THEM!).

I once had a man in my congregation who was also a worship leader, and I would hear reports from others that he was always slandering my worship leading skills or during worship would talk to people around him and share what he would have done differently with this song or that rendition. Once I found this out, I invited him to a nice lunch, treated him, and just humbly asked his advice and for his guidance. Some of his advice was actually pretty good. I got to grow from our conversation, and the very act of taking time to treat him to lunch to let him know he was valued and heard by me changed him as well. We both left that lunch different. Our relationship changed.

From that point on he said hi to me every time he saw me, we got lunch occasionally, and I used that time to build him up (not to try to compete or show I'm a bigger deal, I instantly and happily took a submissive second place!).

Once he *knew* and *felt* I valued him as a musician and a person, he was my biggest supporter. He sat in the front row, shushed people who talked, was the first to start claps, and always texted me after service. Rather than a competitor, he viewed me as a friend, and friends rejoice in their friends' success (primarily because now that they are associated with you, your wins become their wins!)

Now when you come up in a conversation, people like this no longer feel the need to trash talk you to make themselves feel better about their insecurities, they often share of their friendship with you (name dropping) and it just goes to further make them a bigger supporter of you, and for your name to be held in higher regard. And all it cost you was a little double time (and possibly an hour for lunch and a bill!)

Don't look at envious haters as the enemy, but as potentially great and loyal friends who are just a little misguided. Your job is to put in the extra effort, the double time, and win them over. You will not be sorry that you did.

Final Thoughts

There was a lot of information covered in this chapter, and in this book as a whole. There are some helpful things to take away, and fun stories, but at the end of the day, remember what we discussed in Chapter 5. Above all else, remember that first and foremost the only way any of this is possible is by the power of the Holy Spirit.

If you try to do any of this on your own, you will fail. Lean into Jesus and lead like Christ led… faithfully, humbly, and like a gardener.

ABOUT THE AUTHOR

Jared Fujishin was born in the small beach town of Santa Cruz, Ca. He enjoys riding his motorcycle, the mountains, and most of all, time with friends and family spent over good sushi. He was told these were supposed to be written in third person, but it feels very unnatural to him, so if you want more information, you're going to have to twitter stalk him (@jfujishin) or hit him up and ask to share a cup of coffee and talk. (I mean, not like share the same cup, because that would be weird and he's not into that sort of thing.) But he does hope you enjoyed reading and that it will in some way inspire or help you and your ministry! May the Holy Spirit continue to speak to you as you lead your congregation, and bless you as you humbly serve him.

Made in the USA
Las Vegas, NV
10 December 2024